Maybe the Universe Just Isn't That Into You!

Spiritual Responsibility
in a Fluffy Bunny World

Maybe the Universe Just Isn't That Into You!

Spiritual Responsibility
in a Fluffy Bunny World

Colette Brown

Winchester, UK
Washington, USA

First published by Soul Rocks Books, 2013
Soul Rocks Books is an imprint of John Hunt Publishing Ltd., Laurel House, Station Approach,
Alresford, Hants, SO24 9JH, UK
office1@jhpbooks.net
www.johnhuntpublishing.com
www.soulrocks-books.com

For distributor details and how to order please visit the 'Ordering' section on our website.

Text copyright: Colette Brown 2013

ISBN: 978 1 78279 042 6

A CIP catalogue record for this book is available from the British Library.

Design: Lee Nash

Printed in the USA by Edwards Brothers Malloy

We operate a distinctive and ethical publishing philosophy in all
areas of our business, from our global network of authors to
production and worldwide distribution.

Introduction

I am fed up! I could SCREAM! I am demented! Why? Once again I have heard a fluffy bunny excuse as to why things have gone wrong for a person who should know better. It has been a busy week for folk using spiritual excuses for their own bad decisions! Another 'it was a lesson from the universe for me'! Another 'Spirit is taking me in a new direction and I MUST follow'! Another 'My soul lesson was to walk away'!

Why have we given up on personal responsibility? Why can't we just say we made a bad decision and it is haunting us? Or we really WANT to do something? Or that you really need a new direction in life so are just going to go out there and make it happen? Or that a relationship was bad and you found the courage to walk?

Why in recent years do we see the trend to use 'Spirit/ God/ Universe' as an excuse for our own failings or disastrous decisions? What has happened to personal responsibility? Free will? Human error? Risk? And when decisions DO actually work out, how many people actually then give full credit to the Universe? No: then it is all about their own hard work, effort and brilliant ideas. This isn't healthy. This isn't the way of the spiritually evolved. This is just the following of new dogmas in place of old. A spiritual sheep in wolves clothing.

Let me first say a little about myself. I consider myself a spiritual person. I try to walk my talk every day. I follow a shamanic path and try to live in beauty, balance and harmony. Some days I am good at this; others, I am not. But I don't blame the bad days on soul lessons, faulty angel cards, God/Universe/ Spirit. I put blame where blame, if any, is fair. On me! Maybe I simply had a bad day; I was nasty to my husband; I had far too much wine and became too bolshy! I made a decision in haste and now regret it. I chose to over spend, over eat, etc etc… I have had a business that failed and it failed because I went against what my intuition and a damn accurate tarot reading suggested. My fault...and I won't do it again. You could say that was my lesson? Well, it was a costly one and one which was more about my free will and dodgy decision making than any lesson I needed to learn at the time. You see...I am prepared to take responsibility for my actions and not blame the Universe for things that are within my own control. There may be things that are fated to happen to us in life that are part of some sort of greater plan. We have no control over Fate. I believe that these fated events then allow us to show the power of our free will, destiny choices and spiritual evolution. It is in these circumstances that we can rise or fall. It is our choice, and blaming a bad choice on anything other than ourselves is just so disrespectful and even downright delusional.

So, you have seen the books of spiritual affirmations that make every day wonderful and full of fluffy bunny rainbows. You have heard the sound bites and sayings from the gurus. This book is full of spiritual myths debunked, quasi affirmations torn apart, gurus put in their place and arrogant experts exposed. It has offerings to help you live a spiritual life in a human body! Take responsibility for your own life. Don't let anyone woo you with facile compliments. You are not a perfect divinity in a rose coloured aura. You are simply YOU! You are a soul journeying in a very amazing human container. Isn't that enough?

So, here are your 'thoughts for the day', guru words of wisdom and silly sound bites turned on their heads. After reading them, you will be ready to take control of your own destiny and accept the universe as your co-pilot. I hope you laugh. I hope you recognise yourself in some (I did) and can join me in standing up and being counted as spiritual humans evolved enough to take responsibility for our own personal actions. This is not aimed at those who have been severely traumatised, abused, disabled or ill in any way. It is for those of us who have accrued so called spiritual crutches and have begun to live life based on clichés and platitudes. We can all be guilty of this. I have been and sometimes, I still am. I am trying to walk with some sort of balanced outlook though and hope you are too. So it is time to recognise this and cleanse ourselves from the addiction to sound bites, words of wisdom and daily internet aspirations. Detox your spirit and feel free. The answers lie within yourself. Be your own guru!

Spirit is leading me to Timbuktu to truly find myself. I need to go.

Really? Spirit wants you to go the whole way round the world to 'find your inner harmony'? Why can't you do it at home while still being a responsible person to your family and friends? You believe that spirituality is within yourself and that all answers lie within your own subconscious? Then why do you need to travel to find what is inside already? Did you overdose on 'Eat, Pray, Love'?

Can't you resolve to take time out every day for meditation and self awareness in your own home or in nature close by? If you can't find a spiritual connection within then what makes you think that a guru in Timbuktu will have the answers? You will just take your baggage there...and then probably bring it back again. But you will have added financial debt and certain resentment from the folk who had to take up your slack as you waltzed away using Spirit as your excuse.

Do you just need a holiday? Space to think things through? Peace and quiet from teenagers who don't value you? A partner who has become dependent on you?

If you can't find yourself inside your own heart, then moving location isn't going to make a difference! Stay and persevere. Or own up that you simply need time to explore your own spirit. Don't make up a big story when a simple truth is all that is needed.

I have read all the magical books…I am just waiting now for my intents to manifest!

Ah, that wonderful word, 'manifest'. What an all rounder! It means all our dreams will come true; the universe will listen and provide and our deepest desires will be fulfilled. Obviously this is because you have read that 'cosmic ordering true way source of secret insight' book! Or maybe as you say, you have read ALL of them. Then you tried to understand the technique although it was a bit woolly and did your head in. Then you set up your wish board on Pinterest for all to see and help you empower your intent. If all your friends add their energy then that must surely help? You have written your intent, burned it with lavender and sage at the full moon/ new moon with the correct mantra (provided by someone else because you can't do your own) and now you simply have to wait. But meanwhile you have had the secret symbols tattooed onto your forehead and are wearing an elastic band round your wrist that is too tight and will remind you to keep thinking of your intent at all times.

You wander round with a wee smile on your face because lets face it, you must be special if you know the secret! Your aura must look so serene and contented to any worth while aura reader because you now have the understanding of how to communicate with the source of all energy, the divinity within, your heart made soul, the masters, the angels, the Goddess and the man down the fish and chip shop. You have cleared your past demons, cleansed your soul, made amends for past life karma and have been set free and NOW you are waiting for your just reward.

So why hasn't it manifested yet? Oh I hear your excuses. You may have not empowered the intent at the right phase of the moon. You may have not totally cleared your back log of unhealthy attitudes or maybe you need another book? Or maybe the universe just isn't that into you? Maybe you are fine just as you are and all this spiritual too-ing and fro-ing is distracting you from that fact?

I do believe that we can connect with the Universe/God/Spirit and we can be listened too. And yes, intent needs to be done properly with the right frame of mind. This is where a good book on magic can help. It will also not manifest if it simply isn't right for you or your karmic life plan. You are never going to win the lottery if you are meant to experience being poor in this life. You are never going to get that dream job if you don't have the qualifications or the work ethic. Pestering the universe isn't going to help. By all means pray. Do the magic. But back it up with effort and sheer hard work in practical terms. Show that you are willing to make changes, to study, to stop frittering money, to be welcoming to a new but maybe imperfect partner. Maybe then the universe just might come on board!

My mother never showed me affection so now I can't show others how I feel.

That is a shame. I understand that you poor old mum wasn't always appreciative of your colouring in and may have yawned through your nativity play. She may also have fed you beans on toast rather than cook you nutritious vegetables and may have spent her money on lipstick rather than a food blender. She was probably very tired and was juggling her husband, other children and full time job. So when you needed her, she wasn't always fully 'in the moment'. Sometimes you weren't the centre of her universe. How awful for you! But, hey, now you can use that as an excuse for when you don't feel like expanding your own emotional horizons. You can blame your failed relationships on it and walk away quite happily knowing you would fail before you even started. All because your mum wasn't a saint!

Repeat after me... I am an adult now, not a child. I am free to react in whatever way I choose. I can repeat old patterns because they suit me or I can let go of them and live free from the constraints of the past.

I turned my back on organised religion and now walk my own path. I don't do dogma!

Well done! If you weren't happy with the dogma of your organised religion, it is great that you have stood up for yourself and moved away from it. I am happy for you. Unless of course, you stepped away because it was wee bit too hard for you and alternative spirituality looked like an easy option. That is called running away!

Oh, you follow Native American spirituality now? Me too! You have a dream catcher? How nice? Oh…and a Sacred Spirit cd with chants on it? Do you join in with the chants? Do you let them take you on journeys into their meanings and lessons? No…you just like the drums. Ok fine. Have you taken time to read up on the tribal history? Or put yourself in the severe heat of a sweat lodge? Done a vision quest? Do you try to walk in beauty, balance and harmony in everything you do? Do you connect with the seasons and any totem animals? What is a totem animal??? Great Spirit…shoot me now!

Oh! Now you're thinking it would be good to be Hindu? And you think Hinduism isn't an organised religion without dogma? Ahhhh. You have a statue of Shiva and do yoga? Well good luck when Kali Ma comes calling!

Of course if being Hindu doesn't work out for you there is always Wicca, Druidry, Kabala or Chinese mysticism but all have an element of dogma, rules or learning associated with them. Why not simply be an atheist?

We are beautiful, in every single way!

In modern society if you are not conventionally beautiful with a symmetrical face and large baby blue eyes, then sorry, you are not beautiful. This says more about society than you...but the truth is that beautiful people are more likely to get the best jobs and be seen as something to aspire to. This is a fact and one that is responsible for cosmetic procedures, bad body image and shelves of celebrity magazines. So don't stand in front of the mirror with anything other than total honesty or you are simply deluding yourself. Do you really want to be like the male Adonis on the dating site that in real life is puny and pot ugly but can't see the truth? Or the female who doesn't recognise her own face because of all the fillers and Botox? Wouldn't it be better to accept that you are normal? Or unusual? Or even less than a perfect specimen? I am sure you have many talents, can have people laughing at your jokes or can inspire people with your amazing words or deeds? So why do you *need* to be physically beautiful? And if you buy into the conventional beauty myth, then where does that leave people who are disabled or disfigured or racially diverse? If we are judged on modern physical beauty then ninety percent of us are going to fail. So, it is all right not to be beautiful in **every** way. As long as your heart is beautiful, that is all that matters. Fight the stereotype. Don't buy into it by believing that you are what you aren't. You are what you do; not how you look.

My angel cards told me today would be fine and I would have the support of Raphael/ Gabriel/ Uriel to overcome all my problems.

Great...you have now your own personal angel to give you strength in dealing with the annoying call centre customer services department! Or maybe you could just NOT expect an angel to be your prop and decide to fight your own mini battles.

I do believe in angels and have seen a few in my time. They are massive, great awesome beings that scared the hell out of me with their stature and spirit energy. I am not sure I want to see one again! You see each and every time they appeared I was in the deepest despair. I really needed their connection and their affirmation that higher beings do really exist and can lend us their ears from time to time. I so needed to know that something higher could help me in terrible situations. So...yes...I totally believe in angels. I know they are there. But are they really meant to be called on in anything less than real need? Do we need them to oversee our every decision? Or is that not a bit dependent and even disrespectful to them? I would worry that by asking them for daily help that I would annoy them and they might not come when I truly needed them. There is a big difference in using or abusing our spiritual helpers. Ask them for help when you truly need it. If not leave them alone to be fully conscious helpers of someone else who may need their intercession more than you. Practice respect!

By all means pick your daily angel card if it makes you feel better. But use it as a guide and a sense of how an angelic being would help you in taking responsibility for your own decisions. Same with daily tarot, astrological advice, oracle cards, affirmations or thoughts for today. When used wisely and respectfully, these forms of advice can truly help us move forward. But if you are addicted to them and can't make a move without them, then you truly need help.

I keep falling in love with the wrong men/women. You can't help who you fall in love with.

You maybe can't help who you fall in love with but you can sure as hell stop attracting the wrong types into your life. Look at your past loves. Do you see a pattern? Are you a woman who craves the excitement of a dark, intense, soulful man with depressive dark circles and a passion or creativity that drives you wild? Only to realise that they are actual depressives with behavioural problems and no social or life skills? Do you go for known womanisers so you can feel good for a while as you temporarily break their cycle of lust and then send you to despair when they cheat on you with the next willing sap? Do you feel that the nice man who respects you and would make a great long term partner or father to your children as a wee bit boring because he is 'good and nice'? Do you need all the drama to make you feel interesting to your friends? Let's face it...FaceBook would be boring without your distraught updates, wouldn't it? What is it about YOU that is attracting negative types into your life? Think about it and change it!

Are you a man who loves the fact that you can 'save' a vulnerable, fragile woman from her disastrous past but when she becomes strong and hardy will then reject her for 'changing'? Or dump her in case she dumps you because she is strong and maybe doesn't depend on you as much anymore? Or do you seek out a trophy? A beautiful woman who may lack intellect and depth, only to realise later that you crave conversation and opinions? And then you dump her and immediately and fall for the next shallow stunner?

Look closely at what you need and want in a relationship and if it isn't healthy then choose to change those needs. Don't keep falling for every Scorpio with a sting in her tail. Avoid attracting a free spirited Sagittarius if you want a settled nine to five life. You will do yourself no favours by repeating patterns that have never served you well. You can change your outlook and change your unhappiness. It isn't the universe sending you the wrong types. It is purely and simply you putting out signals or being prepared to invest in the wrong people.

I have sensed my spirit guide and he is Native American...it is so special!

That it is! My spirit guide is Native American too but all higher guides are special. To have a higher evolved being come to you to guide you and mentor you is something truly amazing and so potentially illuminating. I thank my Spirit Guide every day for his advice and I know my clients adore him and enjoy being in his presence. He has been with me since birth and he actively takes part in my readings and personal rituals. I am so blessed.

So when did you meet your guide? How did he/she come to you? Oh, you haven't seen him but someone at a psychic fayre drew a picture of him for you. Had you at any time been drawn to Native American spirituality before this? Aahhh...you had a dream catcher and liked Dances with Wolves. Ok...and what do you do in life that needs a higher guide? Are you a healer, clairvoyant, shaman or path worker? No. ok.

In my experience everyone can have lovely family of beings around them and have guidance from above in the form of angelic intervention and ancestor spirits. But to have a higher evolved guide, I do believe that you must be doing some kind of spiritual work whether that be advising, healing or teaching. Other wise, why would you need one?

Let me tell you something about spirit guides that my guide told me and showed me. My guide has been around since as long as I can remember, my wee 'Nindian Boy' who seemed to grow up with me and then became such a wonderful guide in my clairvoyant consultancy. I see him in full winter skins of the Plains Indian and he seemed to stop aging about age 30. This was when he died in his Native American life. One night he took me journeying to show me himself as his true spiritual self. Up and up we flew until we both became simply spirals of white energy. I recognised him no problem but it blew me away and I was very confused when we came back to normal consciousness. He told me that what I had seen had been his true spirit form and I said 'but I thought you were Native American?' He told me that in *one* life he had been and that this was the way he chose to present himself to me from my birth. I asked why and he told me that it was because it was accessible to me and not frightening, as his white light spirit form would have been. He said that I 'know' him as his Native American form and in this way we are connected and work easily together. I asked if other higher guides were the same and he said yes. This means that as a westerner, I would connect with some sort of western spiritual tribe. In this way we can understand why a Chinese healer may connect with a Chinese guide rather than say, a Celtic shaman guide and why an aboriginal Holy Man wouldn't necessarily connect with a Norse guide. They present their spirits in the way that is best for us to access them, not the other way round.

So, all higher guides are special whether they are Native American or Chinese or Celtic etc. This facet of themselves is just a cultural way of making them more acceptable to us. So, rejoice if you do have a higher guide but be very wary of jumping on the bandwagon just because it might make you feel special.

God only ever gives us as much trauma/unhappiness/chaos as we can handle!

Hhhmmm. Try saying that one to the mother whose toddler just died tragically by being strangled by Venetian blind cords! Or to the father whose only son has just been made brain dead by a drunk hit and run driver. Really…go on…and enjoy the slap in the face they give you. And please, let me be there to watch!

Maybe God just gives us life and the chaos and motion of the universe takes care of the rest. Sometimes we are in the wrong place at the wrong time. Life sucks and bad things happen. This does NOT mean that the strong of character are picked out by a truly caring God because He/She knows that they can handle it. This Creator energy could not be so callous to say 'Goodness, they are awful strong so they are the ones I will give the disabled child to…or the incurable disease to. But, see that wee weak and fragile one there…well, they need to be off the hook because they wouldn't handle it. Let me, in my higher power, pick out all the resilient people and land them big fat awful tragedies'.

In dealing with trauma, we can maybe find great strength. We can change things for ourselves and other people. We can find dignity and resilience. But if we want to fall apart, rage at the heavens and fail to see our inner strength, then so be it! If you have had a terrible tragedy in life, you have my deepest sympathy and my support to deal with it in any way that helps you through, as long as it doesn't hurt other people.

I have the answers to all of your life issues in my New Book which is a truly new understanding of how life works at soul level. Follow my path and you will be saved!

There are some really great spiritual self help books out there and some really amazing teachers. Some have very new ideas and some have just have an amazingly clear way of presenting a new take on an old idea. I too have written a book on spiritual help for menopause and aging. I hope it brings a new way of looking at an old tribal way of making the experience relevant to our modern world. This, in its way, I hope makes it slightly unique. But, you see, the ideas and practices have been around for thousands of years. I was just interpreting them for modern age. My book might help women with the experience but I wouldn't say that my words would 'save them'.

You know...the book you are promoting looks great. It has some excellent advice in it. But how much of your thinking is truly new and totally generated by you? And how arrogant you are to assume that your path will somehow 'save' me. The only person who can save me is myself...with a bit of help from them upstairs. If you are so far up your own bahookie to see that...maybe you need to read someone else's book!

I have also read your bio. You see, I want to be sure you really have the answers so it distresses me that you are three times divorced, have a drink driving disqualification, hob nob with Z list celebrities and have a huge unpaid tax bill. These things make me think that, no; you don't have the answers to all my life issues.

Spiritual people can't be fashionable or take care of their appearance.

Spiritual people might be so busy living a very full and intercon-
nected life that may truly not have the time or energy to commit
to fashion or intense grooming. Yet, the idea of the aging hippie
in torn cheesecloth and dungarees truly is a thing of the past.
Spiritual people live in a modern world where a bit of mascara
and spot cover can boost confidence and that's just the men! It
may not be as important to them as to the cast of Jersey Shore but
it can still be a pleasure and an enjoyment. So don't let past
caricatures of smelly tree huggers and warty witches put you off.
There is a new modern bread of spiritually evolved folk out there
that don't stink of patchouli/sweat or go out to the supermarket
draped in crystals. Join us? You can wear your body con dress
and Jimmy Choos if you want. Just make sure you have flats in
your Chanel handbag to run and dodge the envious glances and
spells/intents for manifesting the same.

I am cursed. Nothing has ever gone right for me. I have had nothing but bad luck.

Is this truthful? Has nothing ever gone in your favour? Has life not given you moments of happiness in amongst all your unhappiness? Think about it. We all have times when it looks like the fates are conspiring to lay us low; when every day seems touched by bad luck and chaos. But in life there are always moments of happiness and joy too. Are you sure that you have just not opted out of seeing them? Have you lifted your head recently to look at the wonderful full moon and the stars? Your children's smiles? Your dear funny friends? Have you tried laughing at the chaos and seeing it as something out of your control but which you can choose your reaction to? Because you can! If you truly have had someone nasty put a black curse on you then I do apologise. Visit a respected shaman/ holy person to see if they can remove it. I do think though it is unlikely that you have annoyed someone so much that they have cursed you. In 25 years of practice I have only really seen about 20 cases of dark magic being used against someone. It is more likely that the fates have been a bit against you. But life has a way of balancing out. So now you can look forward to a time when lady luck will be back on your side. If you are clinically depressed you might not see this change. So check with your doctor just in case you need some medical help.

I love psychic readings and go for different ones every week with my friends. It is fun but sometimes they are disappointing.

I don't feel that psychic readings are really meant to be enter-tainment. And having one every few weeks shows that either you have no respect for the paranormal or are actually a 'reading junkie'. You may have genuine wonderful readers who do enjoy their work so much that you get a wee buzz from them and this I suppose makes you feel good. But most readers are there to help you with problems in life or to try to give you proof of the afterlife. They will take their gift very seriously and will not feel good at being thought of as performers. I was most upset recently when my car insurer couldn't find a category to fit my job as a clairvoyant consultant and put me in the category of circus performer'!!! No disrespect to circus performers obviously but it is not what I do.

If you feel the need to visit a psychic every few weeks and feel weird if you miss your daily tarot card online, then maybe you are addicted to readings and need to detox and go cold turkey for a while. It won't do you any harm. In fact, you may find that you deal with issues quite well on your own without outside advice. This will be empowering for you and make you more confident in your own problem solving. Try it?

Also make sure you know what type of reading you need when you visit a psychic. Do you understand the difference between clairvoyant, medium, astrologer, intuitive, angel therapist, shaman etc? Have a wee look at the words below.....

To a clairvoyant:
I always get my Aunty Mary through in a reading. Why didn't she come today?

Because this is a reading with a clairvoyant, not a medium!

To an astrologer:
I always get my Aunty Mary through in a reading. Why didn't she come today?
Sorry, I am an astrologer.

To a genuine medium:
You didn't give me a message from my Aunty Mary. You are rubbish.
Sorry but I can only pass on messages from spirit who make contact and today your Aunty Mary wasn't there. But I do hope you enjoyed the connection with your late father, your miscarried child and I hope you can work with the advice they passed on.

To the fake/deluded medium who thinks they can be as vague as possible:
WOW you are amazing. How did you know I had someone in my family who had a name with the initial 'M' and had a bunch of white flowers for me? I love white flowers. And the description of a wee old woman who wore glasses is just so accurate. I'll be back!
Thanks. Can I take your money now?

Please respect each reader's individual gift and don't expect one thing from them when they clearly work in another way. Give them time to tune into you and don't treat it like a game. Use word of mouth when choosing a reader and please, please if she /he asks you what you are here for, please don't say 'fun'!!!

I hate myself because I am so fat but I can't do anything about it because my fat is a layer of protection.

If you have no underlying physical, mental or emotional issue that is keeping you overweight, then you have to accept that you really can do something about it. It is as simple as energy in must be less than energy out. So you can eat less or exercise more. You can lose weight! Or you can choose to stay overweight and simply stop hating yourself. You can choose to take the consequences of weightiness on your joints, your heart and your physical health. You can choose to accept dying early. Or do something about it. I am overweight. I don't like the fact I get out of puff dancing. I don't like the fact that I can only buy clothes in plus size shops. But I do like nice food, wonderful wine, amazing baking, and am a social eater. I am greedy for the food experience. So I have to accept that trying to lose weight is about balance. If the outcome of better health isn't worth the effort and loss of the joy of food, then don't diet. Be fat. But then don't moan that you can't do anything about it. You can! Eating must just mean more to you than fitness and exercise. Fine! Your choice! Don't lie.

So some guru told you that your layers are protecting you from something deep in your psyche? Well, don't you have a responsibility to find out what that is, work with it and then lose the weight? Otherwise just own up to being a food lover and pass me the cheesecake!

Look at my photos...I am surrounded by ORBS!

Or it could be dust particles behind your camera lens? Reflection from your flash? Reflected light sources in the room? No? It is definitely orbs, you say. Then it must be true!

It is comforting to see proof that your spirit beings or ghosts are around you. We all need to feel that our loves ones visit from time to time and I both believe and know that they do so. And yes, orbs can be seen in various photos that really do have the feel and sense of spirit energy, especially if they are say, around a person's favourite chair or at a family gathering or celebration. In my experience, these orbs have an almost solid look, are circular and seem to emit a real sense of powerful energy. I have seen some with tails that are fast moving and also some that almost seem to show features like the face of the moon. I also believe that more orbs are being caught on digital cameras now than were previously caught on old fashioned ones. This is because of the differences in speed of the photo taking itself (obviously, the technological explanation of this is beyond me and I don't really care!) So yes...more orbs will be caught and this is a good thing!

But, oh dear, it has all gone too far! Now every odd looking white shape or mark is seen as being an orb and as proof that we are literally surrounded by dead folk. So let's take a step back and think rationally. Why would you be surrounded by dead folk? And why so many of them? And in every photo? Were your dead relatives always pushing in to have their photos taken? Were they demented fashion models?

If orbs seem to be appearing a few times in every situation where you take photos e.g. your Christmas celebration, your holiday, your back garden, then it is most likely that you have something wrong with your camera, like a build up of dust under the lens. Sorry to burst your balloon....but this is the simple truth. You know what? You could actually be missing the real thing by assuming every mark is an orb. I am much more interested in seeing photos where there is maybe one solitary orb in a relevant position at a relevant occasion. This could be for example, an orb behind a child at a first Holy Communion maybe indicating that a grandparent who has passed has made the effort to be there. Or an orb at someone's shoulder at the Christmas dinner table giving delight that good old dad made it back for the whiskey toast. Or a very observant orb caught on the professional wedding photos maybe after mum didn't survive cancer long enough to be there. See the difference?

So, by all means keep an eye open for these wonderful examples of spirit energy and enjoy them but please, please stop turning every little white circle into proof that you are loved. You *are* loved by your spirit family. Don't be loved by a watermark!

Everyone has a book in them just waiting to come out!

Maybe; maybe not! You may have the kernel of an idea and the belief that it is totally unique and no one has ever thought of it before and that it will be a best seller. Go surf Amazon and be disappointed. Your idea will normally be there in hundreds of books all competing for sales and peoples attention. This is a hard fact but it is true. If you truly believe in your idea and have a gut feeling about it, then please keep going. If this info puts you off or stops you in your tracks, then you may have a book in you but it isn't going to 'come out'.

The next step is to start putting words down and actually writing your book. This is hard due to day to day commitments like earning a living and those pesky children who need to be fed. Oh, and the partner who might want you in bed when you would be writing at night. Keep going though. Leave the children to fend for themselves, abandon your sex life and go into work with dark circles under your eyes due to lack of sleep. Bit by bit your book will grow and become more solid. If you are not willing to accept possibly negative lifestyle changes for your book, give up. It isn't going to happen.

Still with me? So you have alienated your partner, are a lousy parent and have been reprimanded for falling asleep at work. Your book is now ready and you have lost a year of your life. Now to find a publisher! Oh... you have found one at first go through a newspaper advert promising to take your manuscript and make it a global success? You only have to pay $4,000 for the copy editing and proof reading and another $2,000 for promotion. Well, that's called vanity publishing and you have been caught by your own inflated ego! Do the maths. You may make about 50c a book once it has been published. This means you will have to sell 12,000 books before you make a profit! You could try self publishing but it still isn't inexpensive. You will need to buy your ISBN numbers and keep your e-book price so low that you might not even cover your costs.

So you reject the vanity publisher/self publishing and try to go for a traditional genuine one. Or twenty. And you might then have 19 rejection emails. Your ego will fall to the floor. But that one publisher may want tot take chance on your idea but may suggest that your skills in the written word are not so good and to go back and rewrite it and then they might consider giving you a contract. If you truly love your book, you will do what ever it takes to have your words out there. But years may have passed since the first kernel of an idea. If you decide to keep going and you do gain a contract from a genuine respected publisher then be prepared to work hard. It is a competitive world. You book may sell in low hundreds or low thousands but you know, holding your book will be one of the best experiences of your life. People will read it and be moved by your words. They may learn from you and your experiences. Is all of the above hassle worth it to you though for this outcome? Most authors struggle with their books and very few can give up their day jobs. You need the ideas, the talent for language, perseverance and also a lot of luck. Don't underestimate how difficult the world of publishing is just now. So ask yourself very truthfully…do you really have a book in you and is it *really* just waiting to come out!

I am one of the evolved ones who will ascend at winter solstice 2012.

If you are reading this then we all didn't die and you didn't ascend. What made you think you would? Ahh... that old Mayan calendar again. I know it ended abruptly but maybe the wee Mayan scribe just ran out of ink? Maybe he was having a bad day and wanted a better life/work balance and just had a half day holiday. Then he lost his job for skiving and no one else wanted it because it was a bit heavy with responsibility.

Or maybe there was something amazing about the calendar? Maybe it told of a time when a new age would be heralded in, where the earth would change and maybe, just maybe, people would be more spiritual and full of respect for Her and all beings. As I write this there has been a hurricane on the east coast of USA which left New York flooded and many many folk without electricity. (Haiti and some other wee places were hit too...but they weren't reported as much as they aren't that important!) There have also been recent tsunamis, volcanic eruptions and much general extreme weather patterns in the world. Maybe indeed earth changes have started.

Some Native Americans believe that 2012 to 2074 will be a time of great change for the earth and all who live on her. It will challenge us and may be a time of great austerity. Life will be lost to natural disasters and there may well be more hunger as crops fail and you can't eat an Ipad. So I feel that the Mayan calendar is correct in pinning down a prediction of a big cycle change and we all need to work together to make the world a better place.

How come though, if you are right, that I get to simply die but *you* can ascend? Isn't that what saints and gods/goddesses do? So, you have read a few books, been mentored by a very rich guru and are now ready to transcend from human form to a God form? Wow. I am impressed. Do you ascend with your clothes on or are you like the Terminator and some super heroes that need to find new clothes when they land elsewhere? You don't have answers for that. Well, I am sorry but I would need some practical reassurances about this ascension lark before I signed up. Like where we are all ascending to, how much it will cost and can you go first class? Do we all hold hands as we ascend or is it more like everyone for themselves like that film 2012? Will my cat be able to ascend too? I am too much a of a Taurus for all this. I think I might just die with the rest of the great 'unascended'.

My creativity has come out. I am now a craftsperson!

I am so happy that you have found a way to allow your true creativity to thrive. You must be delighted at the chance to make and create your wonderful crafts. I realise that your day job in the call centre is boring and that this new diversity has allowed you to tap into Spirit in a new and exciting way and I am happy for you. We all need to let our imagination and creativity out. But please, please don't try to sell your wares to me unless you have reached a level of accomplishment that means the sale is valid and doesn't go against the Trades Description Act!

I respect small businesses and buy locally whenever I can. I would rather purchase items from a small manufacturer than a large multinational and I recognise the need to support entrepreneurs and sole traders. This has cost me dearly. Instead of buying wrapped brand name smudge sticks to cleanse my home and for ritual, I bought from you! The pathetic bundles that arrived were weedy, bound wrongly and fell apart at first flame. The feather fan that I thought looked lovely apart from the 'gemstone' stuck on it for no good reason fell apart thankfully before I gave it away as a present. And your dried lavender didn't smell of, well, lavender.

I had a go making my own sage smudge sticks in the past and wasn't very successful. My choice of culinary sage wasn't the most fragrant of offerings. I have also tried to make feather fans, do beadwork for a medicine bag, make a dream catcher and also sew and embroider. All to no avail. My attempts were laughable and very embarrassing so that's why I wanted you to make me things. I could earn my money doing what I am good at and then, in good faith, pass it onto you for your time and talent. This would then allow me time to make home made lemoncello liqueur and write short stories. But this trade wasn't fair. Your goods were faulty and just down right not fit for the purpose. Did I report you? No. Did I complain? No. I am too worried I might upset your sensitive nature and cause you to give up. But someone else will and I hope you still don't give up. I just hope you study your art, practice it and make yourself the best craftsperson you can be. Until then, please don't offer your goods for sale.

I cured myself of cancer. Follow my methods and you too can beat this disease!

Ok...where is your proof? You see, I may be a spiritual person who believes in the power of the mind but I also have a professional qualification as a pharmacist and in my opinion you just can't make big claims like this without the proof to back them up. You may tell me that your diet and/or spiritual outlook cured you, but how do I know that is true? You may believe in your own personal miracle and I am happy for you to do so. I worry about those who take you at your word and maybe decide to fight their own disease on your say so. This is unfair. You say your methods may have cured many others. Again, where is the proof? And what of those who followed your methods and have not been cured? They probably weren't on the phone letting you know. In fact, they may even feel unworthy of talking to you about their 'failure'. Surely it must be their own fault for not following your methods to the letter or starting to follow you early enough? Don't underestimate the fragility of human nature.

People die of cancer every day. Are these people less spiritual than you? What is missing from their souls that you have in abundance? Don't say 'faith'. Don't dare! And certainly don't say that maybe it was just their time to go over especially when you may have given them false hope of life.

Some cancer cells are detected and then with time revert back to normal cells. This can be judged as a miracle for these lucky people. But it is their personal miracle and doesn't mean that they then have the answers for others.

So by all means let people know about how you handled your cancer or disease, what methods you used to help yourself and then leave them to make up their own minds. Please don't say the word 'cure'. It is common knowledge that alternative therapies such as reiki, energy therapies and positive thinking can help a person in their health battles. At least let them fight a fair battle, not one hindered by self doubt because they maybe aren't winning...the way you won.

Anyone can be a clairvoyant/medium/psychic. You just need to open up more.

This is debatable. It is like saying that anyone could learn to play the piano if they practiced enough. However, the end recital may be more 'Chopsticks' than Mozart! This is because of a thing called 'talent'. You can learn new skills, you can practice till your head hurts but if you don't have a God given talent then it may well be, at best, reasonably good and at worst , just mediocre.

Certain people come into this world with certain talents and by developing them and dedicating themselves to them, they will probably be successful with them. This is great. This is right. Equally, a talent wasted or thrown away without developing it does make us feel as though a person has gone against the flow of their life's gift.

You wouldn't assume that you could be surgeon if you had dodgy eyesight, shaky hands, an aversion to blood and had no obvious talent. So why assume that just because you are interested in the paranormal world, that you can buy a tarot deck, put a tea towel on your head and give advice? Even if, as you say, it runs in your family, it might simply have skipped a generation with you.

Look deeply inside. By all means develop yourself to be the best you can. Do the work, learn the techniques. But if after all that you really aren't getting much through in the way of spirits or predictions or psychic understanding, it might be best to simply accept that you have the knowledge but not the talent. Enjoy it for what it is. And what it is, is being a wonderfully intuitive person with enough intellect to know your own limitations.

There are no such things as bad spirits, demons or negative entities. There is only True Love, Light and Positive Energy. Don't be afraid!

How very naive of you! Just because you haven't actually come across negative entities, doesn't mean they aren't there. In this universe, in our world and in the spirit world, there is balance and polarity. That includes dark and light, bad and good. Putting your fingers in your ears and going 'lalalalala' isn't the answer here. I have no proof for you although I have dealt with very negative energies in my shamanic practice and also in my time as a 'ghost buster'. I have had residual pain in my neck where I was attacked by a malevolent spirit. I have been under psychic attack and been pinned to my bed. I have seen many poltergeists. These are my truths but as I have no evidence to support it, I can only tell you of it. So I don't expect you to believe it. I just hope that you may consider it to be possible.

Let's look at myths, legends and world religions. So many of them contain demons, scary monsters, malevolent spirits and mischievous gods and goddesses. Jesus was tempted by a serpent, Durga cut of the head of the buffalo demon, and Loki allowed the mistletoe to kill Balder.

You could say that all these texts and stories are there to allow us to work on our own negativities and fears. But you don't believe in negativity, do you? If there is no such thing as negativity and there is only white light positive energy within us, then why are we given all these warnings?

You say Ouija boards are a safe way to communicate with spirits. No, they are not. Using one is punching a random number into your mobile phone and making the call. You may have someone nice on the end of the line or you may have a serial killer. It's just your luck. So don't go there. I have watched an unknown spirit spell out my dad's name on a board and pretend to be him at a Ouija board demonstration. This spirit knew I could see him yet still showed me his trickery. People do become possessed; grumpy ghosts do haunt houses; poltergeist energy can throw a book at your head. These are not positive energies or entities. So beware. Don't be so sure that one day you won't come face to face with something bad. Believe me, sending it love and light won't work.

If you follow my teachings on natural birth, you won't feel pain and will bond forever in love with your baby.

Dear Lord! Pass me the gas and air! The pain of childbirth is off the scale of any other pain listed and is caused by the muscles of the uterus and birth canal being stretched and opening to a degree that doesn't bear thinking about. This physical trauma must cause pain simply because of the laws of nature. A big bath of warm water, a few chants or some nice smelling oils will not take away that pain. They may help you tolerate it but pain is pain and childbirth is painful. Fact!

I understand where you are coming from and applaud the fact that you are helping many women create a more informal birth where they feel more in control. I don't believe in the culture of 'too posh to push' elective caesareans. I certainly feel everything should be done to help a woman cope with the pain and to help her deliver a healthy child. Ancient tribal techniques of birthing are a good adjunct to modern births. Chanting and focused breathing can help with stamina and coping mechanisms. But they don't stop pain. It is intrinsically impossible to have your vagina stretched to oblivion without it being painful. So stop your nonsense and let women have a safe birth without the pressure of fear of failure. The only failure is when something bad happens and a mum or baby is harmed.

It may be easier to bond with your baby if you aren't woozy after the anaesthetic of a C section. It may be easier to bond if you have managed a birth with out stitches and without heavy, opiate medicines. But it may also be hard to bond with a baby after 37 hours of natural labour with no pain relief and no respite. So forgive me if I am appalled at your statement. If you are saying that you felt no pain whatsoever in a birth situation, then you are either delusional or a man!

My totem animals are eagle and wolf!! They came to me in a workshop where I journeyed with them.

I'll call your 'eagle' and 'wolf' and raise you a 'mountain lion' and 'thunderbird'. Simply journeying in one workshop doesn't make these your spirit totems. They may have been your helpers on this one journey but spirit allies come over a course of time and make their presence felt over months or years. You need to be haunted or hunted by them. Their energy or symbols or photos will turn up everywhere until you realise that something special is going on. You feel them, see them and be given gifts with their image on them and they just eventually won't take no for an answer! When we accept their presence we become empowered with the energy and instincts of that animal ally.

I have run shamanic workshops and have always been a bit sceptical at how many eagles or big cats or wolves come along for the journeying. What about rabbits, otters, mice, snakes, dogs, cats, or guinea pigs? Do they not have validity? In one workshop a very honest student was a bit bemused to be gifted 'mouse' as his spirit animal but he welcomed it and accepted it as he had always been a bit fascinated by the little creatures anyway. 'Mouse' has shown him strength in adversity on many occasions and shown him the power of hard work.

I have always been fascinated by big cats and adore their majesty and elegance. It didn't really surprise me when my main totem showed herself as 'mountain lion' but I also have other totems ranging from rabbit to lizard to spider. These are precious to me and always will be. I am not too proud to admit to being guided by smaller and seemingly less powerful allies. All have a gift of knowledge to give me. There is no spirit ally hierarchy so be wary of your own pride and your own desire for being connected to what you may perceive as superior totems. Be just as ready to accept ant, mole, porcupine or dung beetle as you are the majestic eagle!

I am a practising witch/shaman/druid and take pride in my Path. How dare my line manager reprimand me for dressing inappropriately!

If you have been wearing a delicate pentagram on a fine chain that represents your path, then by all means take it to a tribuneral and sue the bigots! But if you have gone into work dripping in crystals with a huge pentagram pendant and totally kitted out in black velvet with gothic eyeliner, then get grip! Especially if you work as an accountant or civil servant. All professions have dress codes and health and safety guidelines. By all means make sure that you are not subject to prejudice. If the person next to you wearing the huge crucifix hasn't been told off like you...then you have the right to feel maligned if you are wearing something similar of your own faith. The same goes if you have been told off for wearing your small cross or Sikh bracelet.

Many witches and shamans feel that they can dress in any way they please as their religion or path is one of personal freedom. This may be true in your personal life, at home and going shopping but is simply not true in the world of work. We wouldn't expect a teacher to teach looking like he/she was going to do ritual. We wouldn't expect a politician to look like he was ready to camp out to protect a tree. There are certain areas where being conservative is good and the way we dress to work is one of them. Even as a clairvoyant I dress smart/ casual and see no need to be over the top with jewellery etc. I do have my ritual clothes, my ritual jewellery and my feather hair clips. But I keep them special and this actually helps with the aspect of leaving the hectic work world behind and stepping into the world of meditation and honouring. In normal work life remember less is more!

Ego is bad! Lose your ego or you can't be spiritual!

How egotistical of you thinking you can lecture me on my ego! My ego is perfectly fine, thank you! Maybe you need to take closer look at yours!

The ego is a gift from spirit that allows us to feel we matter. It is our way of sensing the way in life, especially in a threatening world where naysayers and negative people can pull us down. It is the spark that says 'I can do this because I believe in myself as a person'. It is the mischievous energy that allows us to take a risk because something inside us believes we are special enough to succeed.

What is bad is an over inflated ego or an ego that is blinkered by self delusion. That is when an ego can be detrimental to our spiritual path, our relationships or life in general. It also makes for great cringeworthy viewing on the X Factor! But having a normal ego is not the same as being a narcissist. That is very different. One helps us to proceed with confidence; the other blinds us into thinking that only the 'I' is important.

If we didn't have an ego, would we ever consider that our talents might be worth exploring? Without an ego, would we ever decide that we are worth more than being in a rotten relationship? Would books ever be written, paintings ever painted or mountains climbed? I don't think so. It is our ego that can persuade us we can do something well and that we are not mediocre.

What about the wee man from the council estate that decided to become a politician? Or the mum who decided to start her own business? Or the disabled athlete who won gold at the Olympics? Or the explorer? Or the actress? Or the bestselling author? See what I mean? So don't let us dispel our egos. Let us nurture them to a degree but also watch they don't over inflate so that we think we can lecture others or tell them what to do!

I am a Rainbow Warrior living the old ways NOW!

Oh give me peace! I have done the survivalist thing; camped in a Tepee; been in the forest with just a Swiss Army knife and I do know how to make fire. These were great experiences and I wouldn't have been without them. But you know, there is something to be said for comfort, warmth and dry clothes. Maybe I am just older now and I need a comfy bed, a kettle and the local shop. This doesn't mean that spiritually I can't walk with my ancestors, take lessons from the past and be environmentally as friendly as I can be. I value simplicity, recycle and support nature. I can do this no bother while working, living and laughing in a modern world.

Spirit gave us gifts of civilisation, metallurgy and spirituality, it also gave us technology. Each gift has been both used and abused. Technology has created great leaps forward for human kind especially in medicine and communications. We have abused this gift by developing weaponry and things like GM crops, but it still can be a source of good.

I have no problem with you living your own lifestyle and enjoying it. But please leave the standing stones where they are; they don't need moving into a better pattern. Also, please realise that your Swiss Army knife isn't an ancient tool and tarpaulin isn't a traditional material. Oh...and your mead tastes of sheep's pee and your rice cakes were made in Bradford!

Be wary of the aliens who live amongst us. And don't trust the government!!

Have you been watching too much 'Men in Black'? Sorry, but wee old Archie next door isn't a lizard type creature from planet Zorbic and his wife doesn't eat human babies for fuel. There aren't giant bunkers underground where aliens have humans captive digging for uranium. We are not plugged into a matrix and you aren't The One!

Science fiction is a wonderful thing; but it is FICTION. Obviously, you will say that you are more intellectual than me and know the truth is out there. Fine, Mulder! I am not disputing the likelihood of life on other planets, that meeting another life form may be coming closer in time or that the government may have some secrets we don't know about. I am open to the thought that the universe is a big place and that we are more than likely not alone. We may even have been visited before as the ancient pyramids and certain myths and legends suggest. Everything is possible but some things are unlikely.

You have more conspiracy theories? I *have* heard that the American moon landing was all a giant hoax too. Possible but not that likely. And Elvis lives next door to you and works in Wal-Mart? Sure! Marilyn Munro was murdered by JFK or the CIA? Oh and those naughty Windsor's had it all planned that Princess Diana should hit a tunnel wall? Next you will be telling me that the American government flew aeroplanes into the Twin Towers so it could win the war on terrorism? Ah ...you were just about to? Sorry... I am bored now but thank you for your insights. Please remember to adjust your aluminium foil hat as you leave your underground bunker, just in case we have to listen to your thoughts.

I was Hitler in a Past Life and that's why I have no friends in this life!

Yes I can see the resemblance! But I would rather think of Hitler burning in hell for eternity than being allowed back to live in a three bedroom semi in a London suburb. Have you thought that you have no friends because you are simply not that friendly to others? Ahhh...that's how Hitler started out too? I see now. Please shut the door as you leave.

In many years of doing past life readings I can honestly say that I have never come across a Cleopatra, Hitler, Merlin, Joan of Arc or Jesus. Most past lives are about living in a certain place, with a certain group of soul family members and friends and maybe a soul mate. The Past Life lessons are normally about interrelationships and how you can make progress in this life. They can also be about repeating talents, spirituality and also about bad decisions. They can be traumatic and leave memories which are negative and can hold us back in this present life.

But please don't get above yourself. By all means, if you have an interest in past lives then read up on it, think on it and if you are fascinated then by all means have a past life reading or professional regression. These may help you with any issues that keep repeating in your life or give you an understanding of the depth of feelings you may have for a certain person. Just go with an open heart and don't expect to be some one famous in history. Or you might just find out that you were an 18th century harlot rather than a vestal virgin!

Final Words

If you have seen some versions of yourself in the previous pages you may be having one of two reactions. You could be thinking 'what an arrogant woman the writer is and how dare she poke holes in what is dear to me'. I have done this possibly because so much of the content is also dear to me! Or you could find yourself agreeing with some of the points made and resolve to change your dependency on sound bites and on words of wisdom that too often trip off the tongue without real thought behind them.

If you hated the book, well thank you for at least reading so far. If it resonated with you then maybe there has been a sense of disquiet in you anyway and now you can listen to it fully.

I have had many wonderful mentors and teachers in my life. Not one has ever forced or coerced me into anything. In fact, instead of answering my questions, they sometimes left me with more. A good teacher will simply show you their way. And yes...that might be through a book or a workshop that you have to pay for. Teachers and spiritual 'full timers' need to eat and pay their rent. There is no issue about handing over money to someone genuine who will share their knowledge. This is different to a guru who will tell you what you have done wrong and how his/her way will bring you your hearts desire.

If you are planning your day because of a computer generated horoscope, waiting for your daily tarot/angel/oracle card before you can go to work or simply leaving your decisions to someone who isn't yourself, then you need to detox. You need to carefully listen to your own thoughts and yes, your own wisdom.

If you have used some of the excuses above then it is simply time to pull back and take full responsibility for your own actions. In doing so you will be free then to enjoy the feelings of success that come from using your free will to its best advantage.

I am not asking you to never have a tarot reading (I would be out of a job if you did) but have one a year or when you really need one for clarity and don't ponder over your own cards every day. Let spontaneous affirmations guide you e.g. those from a relevant song coming on the radio. If any advice fills you with a bit of unease, listen to your own intuition. If any solution seems too good to be true, then maybe it is?

Some but not all sound bites, articles or quotes will have sound teachings behind them. Remember too that some can be taken out of context and become something that was never intended by the author. So much of the New Age movement is founded on such sound principles that it is terrible to see the way they have been manipulated, changed and used for personal gain or simply muddled due to the need for ever more spiritual chatter. I do not intend to offend anyone with this book but I do feel that if you are offended in any way, maybe it is time to look closely at any caricatures in this book and see if you are starting to resemble them. Then step back, think deeply and make the changes that can bring you back into balance and away from being a spirituality junkie.

Life is a great mystery. If we had all the answers, it wouldn't then be a great mystery and we would have nothing to learn. Take your power back and stand up for yourself. Spiritual responsibility is your right. I'll leave you with a sound bite and a fact: Responsibility is just the ABILTY to RESPOND and not every white feather dropped comes from an angel!

Acknowledgements

Many thanks to my husband Jim for catching me in the moment and suggesting my rants against spiritual irresponsibility would make a great wee book. I am giving you the praise so I can also kill you when I lose half my facebook followers and annoy some clients, friends and fellow professionals!

Thank you to my daughters Jennifer and Jillian who genuinely support everything I do. Thank you Sooz and Malcolm, Becca and Lauren, my spirit family for support and cocktails.

I would also like to thanks Alice Grist for her belief in this book and Soul Rocks Books for making it happen. Many thanks go to John Hunt Publishing for making my dream come true with the publication of my four books.

I would like to thanks some friends who have been so supportive of my writing: Hazel and Allan, Lesley, Hilton, Stevie, Mark, Susan, Maria, John and Michele, Tom and Margo and all at The Motherwell Times.

I would also like to say I have the best clients in the world.

Soul Rocks is a fresh list that takes the search for soul and spirit mainstream. Chick-lit, young adult, cult, fashionable fiction & non-fiction with a fierce twist